KNOWABOUT
Length

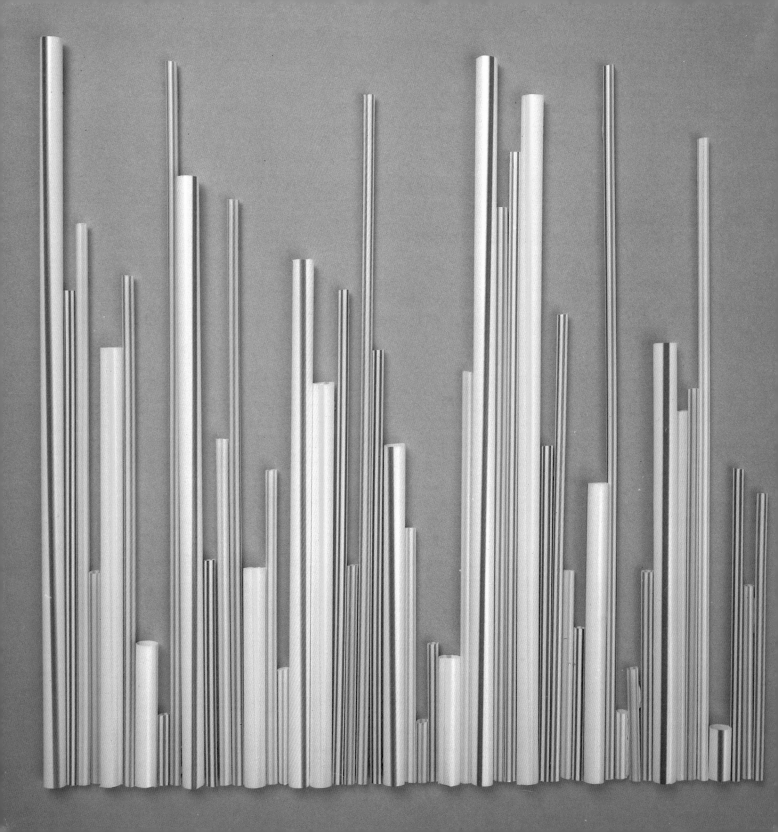

KNOWABOUT
Length

Text: Henry Pluckrose
Photography: Chris Fairclough

Franklin Watts

London/New York/Sydney/Toronto

© 1988 Franklin Watts
12a Golden Square
London W1

Reprinted 1989, 1990, 1992

ISBN: 0 86313 654 0
Editor: Ruth Thomson
Design: Edward Kinsey

Typesetting: Keyspools Limited
Printed in Hong Kong

About this book

This book is designed for use in the home, playgroup, and infant school.

Mathematics is part of the child's world. It is not just about interpreting numbers or in mastering the tricks of addition or multiplication. Mathematics is about ideas. These ideas (or concepts) have been developed over the centuries to help explain particular qualities, such as size, weight, height, as well as relationships and comparisons. Yet all too often the important part which an understanding of mathematics will play in a child's development is forgotten or ignored.

Most adults can solve simple mathematical tasks by "doing them in their head". For example, you can probably add up or subtract simple numbers without the need for counters, beads or fingers. Young children find such abstractions almost impossible to master. They need to see, talk, touch and experiment.

The photographs in this book and the text which supports them have been prepared with one major aim. They have been chosen to encourage talk around topics which are essentially mathematical. By talking with you, the young reader will be helped to explore some of the central concepts which underpin mathematics. It is upon an understanding of these concepts that a child's future mastery of mathematics will be built.

These shoe laces are not the same.
Each lace is a different length.

Which lace
would be best
for this boot?

Which lace would be best
for this shoe?

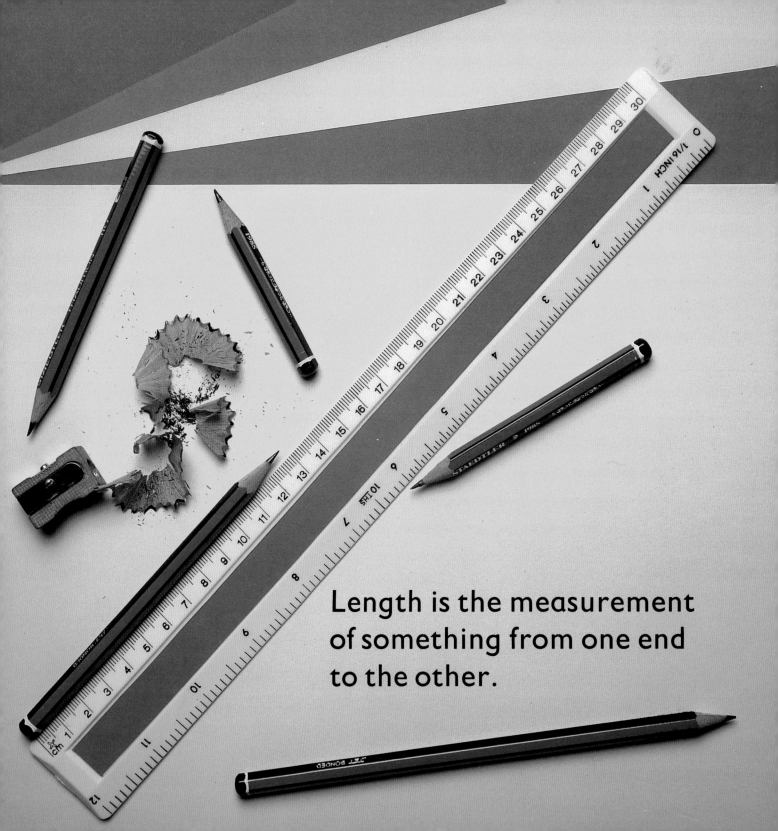

Length is the measurement of something from one end to the other.

We talk about the length of a swimming pool ...

the length of a running race . . .

and the length of a motorway.

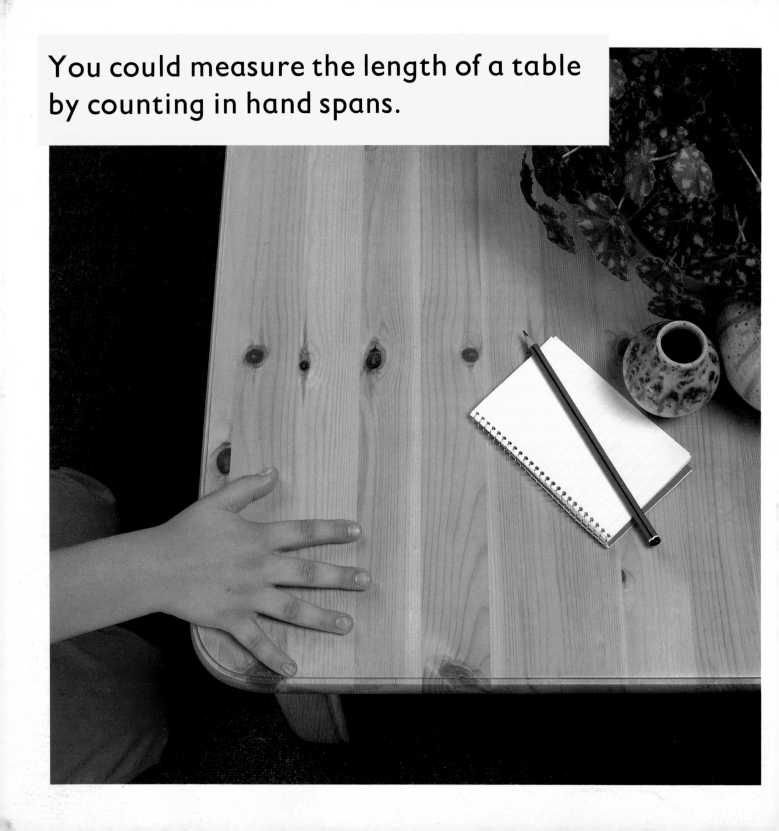

You could measure the length of a table by counting in hand spans.

You could measure
the length of a wall
by counting in paces.

But people's hands are not all the same size . . .

and their paces may be different lengths.

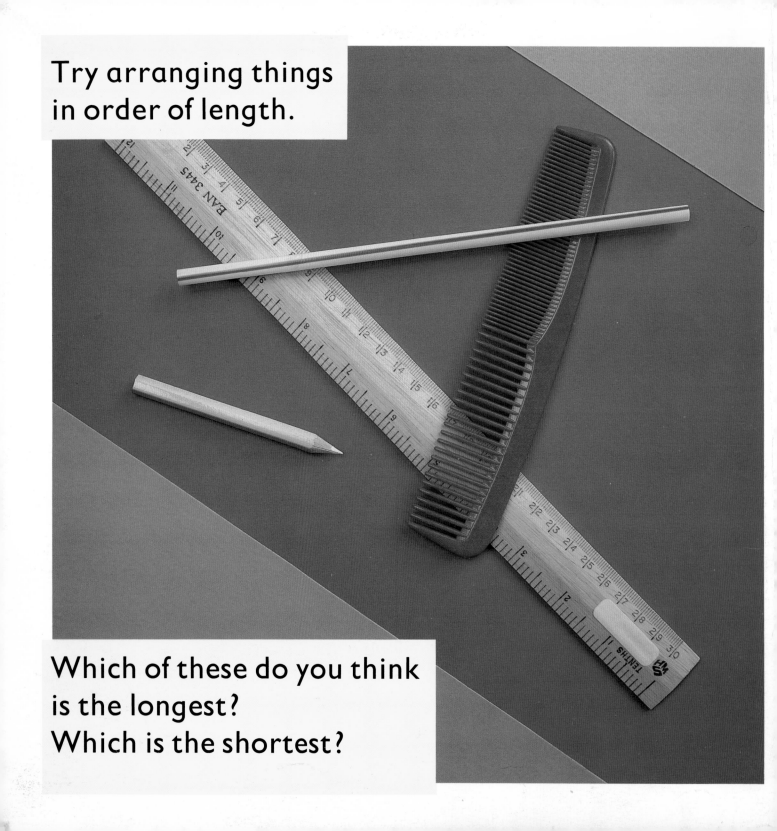

Try arranging things in order of length.

Which of these do you think is the longest?
Which is the shortest?

You could try guessing.

Arrange them like this
to check whether your answer
is correct.

To make exact measurements
we use standard measures.
They are the same everywhere.

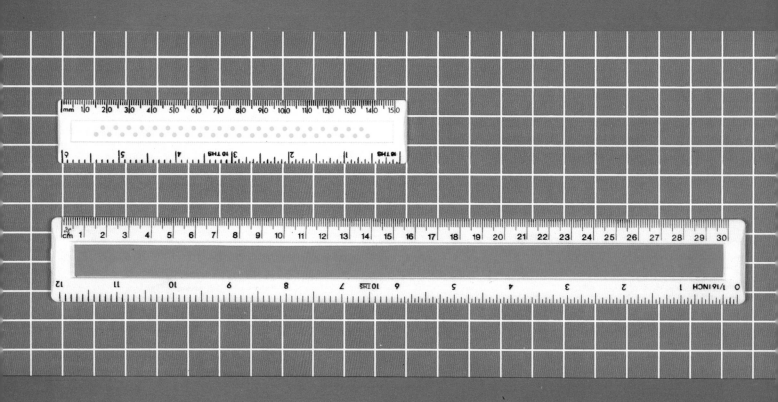

Small lengths are measured
in centimetres.

Longer lengths are measured in metres.

Standard measures are useful
for cutting an exact amount of wood . . .

or an exact amount of cloth.

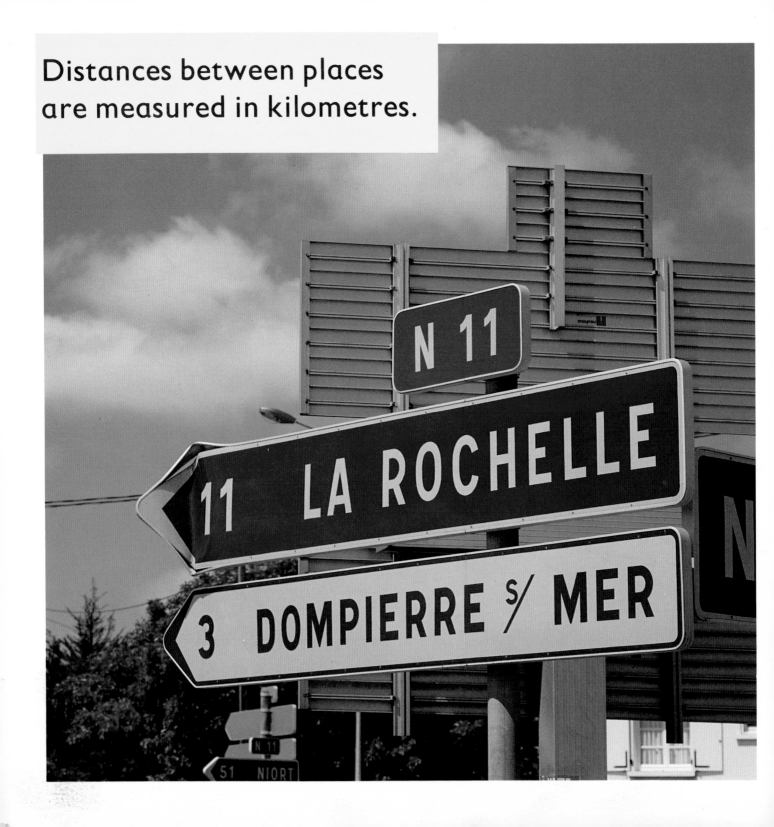

Distances between places are measured in kilometres.

We also use
standard measures
to measure height.
What is your height?

Height is the measurement
from the top of something
to the ground.

You could measure the height of the stick
and the length of its shadow.

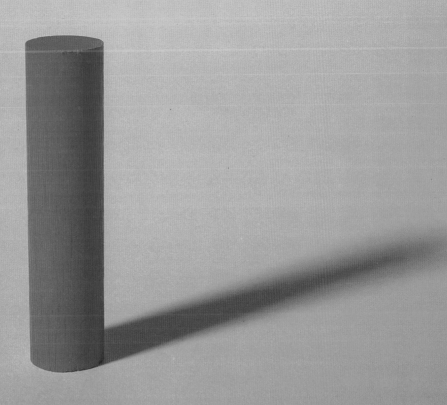

Do you think that the height of the stick is greater than the length of the shadow?

What is the difference
between height and length?

How high can you jump?

How far can you jump?

We can compare the height of things with our own size.

Build some towers
like this.

Can you arrange them
in order of height?